World Crafts and Recipes

Recipe and Craft Guide to

SOUTH AFRICA

Melissa Koosmann

Mitchell Lane

P.O. Box 196
Hockessin, Delaware 19707
Visit us on the web: www.mitchelllane.com
Comments? email us: mitchelllane@mitchelllane.com

Mitchell Lane
PUBLISHERS

World Crafts and Recipes

The Caribbean • China
France • India • Indonesia
Israel • Italy • Japan • **South Africa**

Copyright © 2012 by Mitchell Lane Publishers

All rights reserved. No part of this book may be reproduced without written permission from the publisher. Printed and bound in the United States of America.

PUBLISHER'S NOTE: The facts on which the story in this book is based have been thoroughly researched. Documentation of such research can be found on page 60. While every possible effort has been made to ensure accuracy, the publisher will not assume liability for damages caused by inaccuracies in the data, and makes no warranty on the accuracy of the information contained herein.

To reflect current usage, we have chosen to use the secular era designations BCE ("before the common era") and CE ("of the common era") instead of the traditional designations BC ("before Christ") and AD (*anno Domini*, "in the year of the Lord").

Library of Congress
Koosmann, Melissa.
  Recipe and craft guide to South Africa / by Melissa Koosmann.
    p. cm. — (World crafts and recipes)
  Includes bibliographical references and index.
  ISBN 978-1-61228-080-6 (library bound)
  1. Cooking, South African—Juvenile literature. 2. Handicraft—South Africa—Juvenile literature. 3. Cookbooks. I. Title.
TX725.S6K66 2012
641.5968—dc23

                                          2011031007

eBook ISBN: 9781612281674

Printing   1   2   3   4   5   6   7   8   9

                                          PLB

CONTENTS

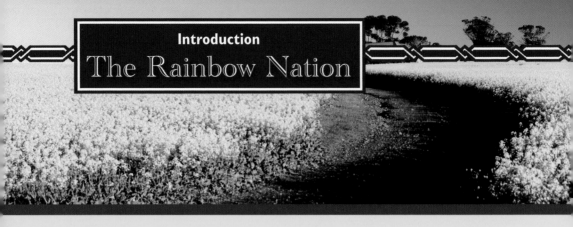

South Africa, a large country of 50 million people at the southern tip of Africa, is sometimes called the Rainbow Nation because it is so diverse. The majority of South Africa's citizens are black Africans, but large minorities are white, Indian, Asian, or members of the mixed-race group that South Africans call coloured.

Partly because of this diversity, there is no one typical South African way of life. Instead, the country encompasses many contrasts. Traditional cultures exist side-by-side with modern ones. People celebrate Christian, Muslim, and traditional African holidays. Some South Africans live in large houses with all the comforts of modern life. Others live in traditional African huts, or in shacks constructed from corrugated metal and plywood, often without running water or indoor toilets.

For much of South Africa's recent history, virtually all of its wealthiest citizens were white. Only white people were allowed to vote or participate in the country's government, and they made laws that favored their own race over others. For about half of the twentieth century, they codified these laws into a system called apartheid that kept people of different races strictly separated.

In 1994, however, South Africa became a democracy, and every citizen was granted equal rights. Today, South Africa's people are trying hard to heal from their country's history of racial injustice. They are working to overcome challenges such as crime, high rates of HIV/AIDS, political corruption, and poor education. South Africans of various races are learning to get along together, and more and more black South Africans are advancing into the country's middle and upper classes.

Long before South Africa achieved freedom, the country's many cultures began mixing together on the dinner table. This book includes traditional African recipes as well as recipes brought to the country by immigrants from

South Africa

- ----- International Boundary
- ----- Province Boundary
- ★ National Capital
- ◉ Province Capital

Railroad
Expressway
Road
Rivers

```
0    100    200    300 Kilometers
0    100    200    300 Miles
```

ZIMBABWE

Plumtree

Francistown

Rutenga

Rio Sav

BOTSWANA

Selebi Pikwe
Beitbridge
Chicualacuala

Mahalapye
Messina

MOZAMBIQU

Limpopo

NORTHERN
PROVINCE

Pietersburg
(Polokwang)

Limpopo

Chokwe

Kalkrand

Gaborone
Nylstroom

Nelspruit

Xai-X

Mariental

Lobatse

Rustenburg

Pretoria

MPUMALANGA

Mapu

NAMIBIA

Tshabong

NORTH-
WEST

Mmabatho
Johannesburg

Witbank

Mbabane

GAUTENG

SWAZILAND

uanien

Keetmanshoop

Vryburg

Klerksdorp

Vereeniging

Standerton

Golela

Seeheim

Hotazel

Vaal

Kroonstad

KWAZULU-
NATAL

Ulundi

Karasburg

Sishen

Bethlehem

Ladysmith

Upington

FREE
STATE

Richards Bay

Orange

Kimberley

Tugela

olloth

Springbok

Orange

NORTHERN
CAPE

Bloemfontein

Maseru

LESOTHO

Pietermaritzburg

SOUTH
AFRICA

Mafeteng

Durban

OUTH
LANTIC
CEAN

Calvinia

Vanrhynsdorp

Victoria West

De Aar

Middelburg

Orange

Kokstad

Port Shepstone

Umtata

EASTERN
CAPE

Queenstown

INDIAN
OCEAN

Saldanha

Beaufort
West

Bisho

East London

Cape Town

Worcester

WESTERN
CAPE

Swellendam

Mosselbaai

Port Elizabeth

Cape of
Good Hope

Cape Agulhas

INDIAN OCEAN

Where in the World

around the world. Whether the foods were invented in South Africa or not, almost all have been changed by the tastes, ingredients, and traditions of the Rainbow Nation's many cultures.

South African foods contain many spices. Main dishes tend to be slightly sweet, often with a hint of cinnamon. Much of the country is good for raising sheep, so lamb is a common—and relatively inexpensive—meat.

Tips for the Kitchen

Read through the recipe—*all the way*—before you start.

Wear an apron to protect your clothes.

Wash your hands with warm water and soap before you start and after handling raw meat.

Be careful! Always get help from **an adult** when you are using the oven, the stovetop, or sharp knives. Use oven mitts to lift hot lids, baking sheets, and pans. Protect the counter with a trivet before you set down a hot container.

Clean up right away.

Use kitchen gloves and avoid touching your face when handling raw chili peppers. The chili juice and seeds can burn your skin.

Once you've made a recipe successfully, you can experiment the next time. Change the ingredients. Add different kinds of fruits and vegetables, or substitute brown sugar for honey.

Finally, share your food with your friends and family. Seeing people enjoy your cooking is as much fun as enjoying it yourself!

A South African braai with sauces

Seafood is also popular, and South African restaurant menus feature many local fish that cannot be found in the United States.

The crafts presented in this book reflect the diversity of South Africa's people, the richness of its history, and the challenges of contemporary life. They will help you explore the history of southern Africa's earliest inhabitants and learn a bit about the Europeans who came to the area. You will make some crafts that South Africans make today, and you will try some activities that South Africans enjoy. Take a lively, flavorful trip through this vibrant country, from prehistory to modern times.

Rock Art

The San people, the oldest known inhabitants of southern Africa, were hunters and gatherers. They painted pictures, some quite detailed, of people and animals on rock overhangs where they cooked and slept. Much of this prehistoric art still exists in South Africa.

The San's paintings probably held moral or spiritual importance. Many of their pictures show ceremonies involving people dancing or hunting with spears. Paintings of animals feature eland, the largest antelope in southern Africa, as well as African animals you may find more familiar, such as elephants, zebras, and giraffes.

Most San paintings are red, yellow, or white. Archaeologists think the San made paint by grinding up rocks called white limestone, red ochre, and yellow ochre, then mixing the resulting powder with blood or animal fat.

You can use similar colors of store-bought paint to make your own rock art. If you like, you can imitate the San and paint African animals or dancing people. Or you can paint pictures of people, animals, and objects that are important to you.

Materials:

Large rocks
Pencil for practice
Red, white, and yellow
    tempera paint

Paintbrushes
Containers for paint
Old T-shirt or apron
    to cover clothes

Instructions:

1. Ask **an adult** where you can collect some large rocks. You might look in your own backyard or in a vacant lot or parking lot near your home. You might also collect rocks at a local park or beach, but if you do this, please check first to make sure you are not breaking any rules. Pick out rocks that are big enough to hold a whole picture but small enough to carry. Get at least two or three rocks so that you can try out various ideas and also start over if you make a mistake.

2. Wash your rocks to remove dirt and moss. Allow them to dry.

3. If you wish, draw your ideas on the rock's surface with a pencil before you start to paint.

4. Paint pictures on your rocks.

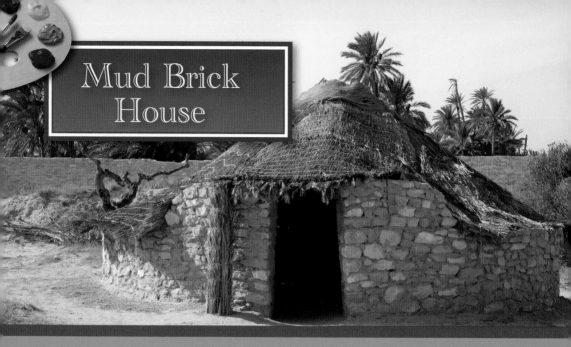

Mud Brick House

Southern Africa has been a multicultural place for at least 1,500 years, ever since Africans who spoke a family of languages called Bantu languages began moving into the territory that was inhabited by the San. Unlike the nomadic San, Bantu-speaking Africans were farmers. They grew crops, herded animals, and built permanent homes.

Today, a few South Africans still live in the kinds of houses their ancestors built 1,500 years ago. One common style of house is a round hut, often made from a mixture of mud, grass, and animal dung. Roofs are made from dry grass, called thatch, which provides insulation and keeps water out. You can use clay and cardboard to make a model of one of these houses.

Ingredients:

Clay
Corrugated cardboard
Scissors
Paper
White glue

Instructions:

1. Choose a large, flat piece of cardboard to make a platform for your house. Mold your clay into a round house shape. Don't forget to make a door.

2. To make the roof, choose another piece of cardboard. Peel the paper off both sides to reveal the folded corrugations underneath. You will use this material for your thatched roof, but first you need to make a cone base to support it.

3. With your scissors, cut out a circle of paper. It should be about an inch wider than the top of your mud hut.

4. Make one straight cut from the edge to the center of your circle of paper. Glue it into a cone shape.

5. Cut triangles of corrugated cardboard and glue them down on top of your paper cone, covering it completely. Let it dry.

6. When you are finished, place your roof on top of your finished house.

Millet Porridge

Before Europeans arrived in southern Africa, the staple food was a small grain called millet. Millet was as important to these farmers as starches like bread, potatoes, and corn are to us today. People ate the grains whole or ground, toasted or boiled. They even used them to make a drink like beer.

You can find millet at health food stores. This simple porridge works as a breakfast meal or as a side dish for lunch or dinner.

Prep time: 5 minutes
Cook time: 30 minutes
Serves: 4

Ingredients:

1 cup millet
4 cups water
A pinch of salt
Honey or fruit

Instructions:

1. Mix the millet, water, and salt in a pan. Ask **an adult** to bring the pan to a boil.
2. With the help of **an adult**, reduce the heat and cover, letting the pan simmer for 30 to 35 minutes, until the millet grains are soft.
3. Remove the porridge from the stove and serve it with honey or fruit.

Message Bracelet

Southern Africans have a long history of creating beautiful beadwork. Traditionally, people made beads from materials like seashells, ostrich egg shells, animal bones, and metal. They also traded for beads brought to the region by Arab traders and European explorers.

Among a large South African cultural group called the Zulus, beads are a form of communication. The colors of the beads and shapes of the arrangements can pass subtle messages.

Consult the following chart to learn the meanings for various colors of beads. The white beads have entirely positive meanings, but the other colors on the list have both positive and negative meanings. It is okay to choose just one or two of the meanings for each color as you make your bracelet.

White	Truth, wholesomeness, spiritual love, and good luck
Blue	Faithfulness, the sky or sea, and sometimes dislike or gossip
Red	Passion, blood, anger, and sadness
Green	Environment, peace at home, and sometimes jealousy
Yellow	Wealth, fertility, and sometimes illness
Black	Sadness, loneliness, disappointment, and death

Memory wire
Wire cutters
Needle-nose pliers
Colored beads of choice

Instructions:

1. Decide how long you want your bracelet to be, and, with the help of **an adult**, use the wire cutters to cut the memory wire to that length. When in doubt, give yourself a little extra wire. You can always trim your bracelet shorter at the end.
2. Use the needle-nose pliers to crimp a small loop at one end of the wire. The loop should be just a little bigger than the holes in the beads to stop the beads from slipping off as you string them. This step can be difficult, so ask an adult for help if you need it.
3. String beads onto your wire. Think about the Zulu meanings for the beads as you work.
4. When you think you have enough beads for a complete bracelet, trim the wire if necessary. To finish the bracelet and prevent the beads from falling off, use the pliers to make a second small loop at the open end.

Sextant

Polaris

Ursa Minor

Europeans first visited southern Africa in the late 1400s, when the Portuguese sailors Bartolomeu Dias and Vasco da Gama led expeditions around the Cape of Good Hope. A century and a half later, in 1652, the Dutch began building a settlement on the site of present-day Cape Town. This settlement would provide supplies to passing trade ships.

Accurate knowledge of the stars was extremely important for sailors because it helped them figure out where they were. Beginning in the 1700s, sailors used a tool called a sextant to determine their latitude, or how many degrees they were distant from Earth's equator. In the northern hemisphere, sailors generally used Polaris, the North Star, to figure out their latitude. But South Africa is in the southern hemisphere, and Polaris is not visible there. Because of this, sailors in the area had to calculate their latitude by measuring the angle of the sun at exactly noon.

Ursa Major

Materials:

Square of cardboard about
    6 inches by 6 inches
Pen or pencil
Protractor
Scissors
Button
Coin
Clear tape
String, about 8 inches long
A plastic tube from a
    ballpoint pen

A sailor using a sextant

Instructions:

1. On the cardboard, draw a straight line from side to side, about ½ inch from the bottom edge. Draw another straight line from the top to the bottom, about ½ inch from the left edge.
2. Poke a hole through the cardboard where the two lines meet.
3. Place the center of your protractor on the hole you just made. Use the protractor to mark the angles, at 5- or 10-degree intervals, from 0 degrees to 90 degrees, on the cardboard. Cut off the excess cardboard beyond these marks.
4. Thread one end of your string through the hole in your cardboard so that about one inch pokes out

the back side (the blank side). Tie this tail to the button to prevent the string from slipping out of the hole.
5. Tape the coin to the long end of the string to create a weight.
6. Tape the tube from your ballpoint pen along the 0-degree edge of the cardboard, as shown.

7. Take your sextant outdoors and take a peek. What do you see?
8. On the next clear night, go outside and find Polaris, the North Star. If you look through the pen at Polaris, the string will hang down, weighted by the coin, and show you your latitude. If you're not sure how to find the North Star, you can look up detailed instructions in an encyclopedia or online.

Never look directly at the sun. Do not use your sextant to find the height of the sun.

Pap and Veg

Prep time: 30 minutes
Cook time: 30 minutes
Serves: 6

After European settlers brought corn to southern Africa, this crop quickly replaced millet as the most important starch. Few South Africans eat millet today. Instead, corn is the star player in many foods we now think of as traditionally African.

One of the most common South African corn dishes is mielie pap, a thick porridge made from white cornmeal. People eat mielie pap with almost anything, including this simple vegetable dish.

Ingredients:

Spinach
1 large bunch spinach
2 tablespoons olive oil
1 teaspoon whole cumin
1 teaspoon whole coriander
¼ teaspoon salt

Squash

1 butternut squash
¾ cup water
2 tablespoons butter
1 cinnamon stick
2–3 cardamom pods
½ teaspoon ground cumin
½ teaspoon ground coriander
¼ teaspoon turmeric
½ teaspoon salt

Mielie Pap

3 cups water
½ teaspoon salt
1–2 cups white cornmeal

Instructions:

Spinach

1. Wash and chop the spinach.
2. Put the olive oil in a pan and, with the help of **an adult,** heat it over medium heat. Add the spinach and spices. Cook covered for 5 to 10 minutes.

Squash

1. Peel the squash and chop it into 1-inch cubes.
2. Place it in a covered pan with the water, butter, and spices. Ask **an adult** to help you bring it to a boil.
3. Turn down the heat and let it simmer for about 20 minutes.
4. When the squash is very soft, ask **an adult** to help you take it off the heat. Mash the squash into a paste with a wooden spoon.

Mielie Pap

1. Bring the water and salt to a boil.
2. Turn the burner down to low heat. With **an adult's** help, add the white cornmeal gradually, about a quarter cup at a time. Stir constantly. Continue to add cornmeal until the mixture gets very thick, like stiff mashed potatoes. When it reaches that thickness, keep stirring and cooking the mixture for another 2 to 3 minutes.

Serving Pap and Veg

Serve your mielie pap with the spinach and squash on top. You may want to remove the cinnamon stick and cardamom pods before you begin to eat.

Bobotie

When Dutch settlers began building Cape Town, slavery was still a common practice. Settlers brought slaves to the colony from Southeast Asia and from other parts of Africa. Slaves, who did most of the cooking for settlers, mixed their Asian cooking knowledge with Dutch food traditions and local African ingredients. In the process, they invented a new food tradition, now called Cape Malay cuisine, which features many heavily spiced, slightly sweet main dishes.

This ground beef dish, called bobotie, looks a little like meatloaf—but the unique mixture of Cape Malay spices makes it taste much better!

Prep time: 10 minutes
Cook time: 60 minutes
Serves: 4

Ingredients:

1 large onion
2 tablespoons oil
1 pound ground beef
1½ cups milk
3 slices bread
⅓ cup raisins

1 teaspoon apricot jam
3 teaspoons hot chili sauce
2 teaspoons curry powder
2 eggs, beaten
Salt to taste
Black pepper to taste

Instructions:

1. Preheat the oven to 350°F.
2. Chop the onions and, with **an adult**'s help, cook them in the oil. When they are soft, move them into a bowl.
3. Ask **an adult** to brown the ground beef, drain it, and add it to the bowl with the onions.
4. Soak the bread slices in the milk briefly. Remove them, squeeze out the excess milk, and set the milk to one side. Crumble the bread into the bowl with the onions and meat.
5. Add the raisins, jam, chili sauce, and curry powder and mix well.
6. Place the meat mixture into a greased medium-sized baking dish. Bake for 30 minutes.
7. When the meat mixture has been in the oven for 20 minutes, ask **an adult** to help you heat the milk in a small pan over low heat. Take it off the heat when it begins to steam. Do not let it boil. Mix the milk with the eggs and add salt and pepper.
8. With **an adult**'s help, remove the meat from the oven and pour the egg mixture over it. Return it to the oven and bake for 15 to 20 minutes, until the egg is cooked.

Koeksisters

Sweet foods are popular in South Africa, so naturally Cape Malay cuisine includes desserts as well as main dishes. One of the most common desserts is a kind of doughnut called a *koeksister*. There are many versions of this dessert, but one of the most common is made of braided dough, which is deep-fried and coated in syrup.

You will need to make the syrup and dough separately. If possible, make the syrup the day before and let it cool in the refrigerator overnight.

Ingredients:

Syrup
3 cups sugar
1 cup water
1 teaspoon ground ginger
3 cinnamon sticks
Juice of 2 lemons

Dough
1¾ cups flour
½ teaspoon salt
2 tablespoons baking powder
3 tablespoons butter
1 egg
⅓ cup water
Vegetable oil for frying

Instructions:

Syrup
1. Mix all the syrup ingredients together, dissolving the sugar in the water and lemon juice.
2. With **an adult**'s help, heat the mixture slowly. Start on low heat and increase gradually to high heat until the mixture begins to boil. Watch your pot constantly during this step. If you are not careful, the pot will boil over.

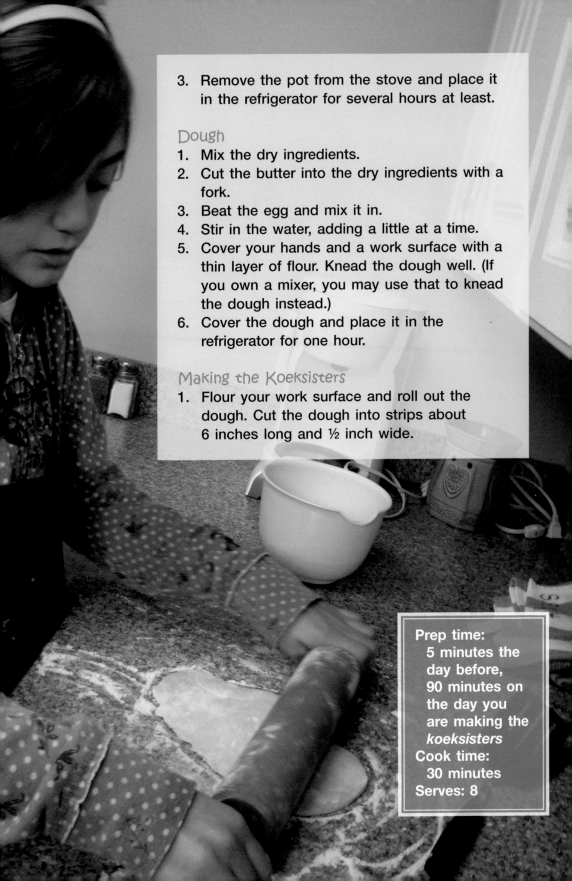

3. Remove the pot from the stove and place it in the refrigerator for several hours at least.

Dough
1. Mix the dry ingredients.
2. Cut the butter into the dry ingredients with a fork.
3. Beat the egg and mix it in.
4. Stir in the water, adding a little at a time.
5. Cover your hands and a work surface with a thin layer of flour. Knead the dough well. (If you own a mixer, you may use that to knead the dough instead.)
6. Cover the dough and place it in the refrigerator for one hour.

Making the Koeksisters
1. Flour your work surface and roll out the dough. Cut the dough into strips about 6 inches long and ½ inch wide.

Prep time:
5 minutes the day before, 90 minutes on the day you are making the *koeksisters*
Cook time:
30 minutes
Serves: 8

2. Take three strips of dough and press them together at one end. Braid them and press them together at the other end. Repeat this process until all the dough is braided.

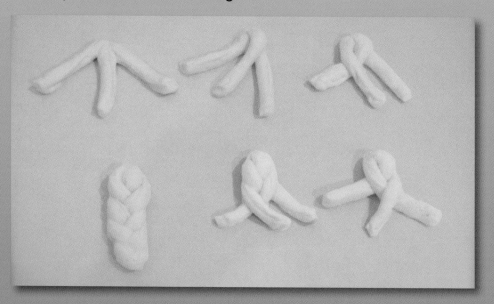

3. Fill a large pan with 2 inches of vegetable oil and heat it over medium heat. While it heats, remove the syrup from the refrigerator and place it in a large bowl.

4. Ask **an adult** to help you deep-fry the *koeksisters.* They should stay in the oil until they turn a deep golden brown.

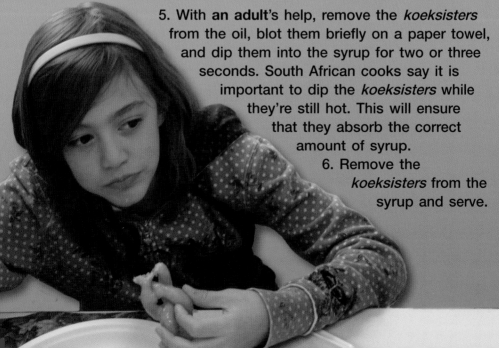

5. With **an adult's** help, remove the *koeksisters* from the oil, blot them briefly on a paper towel, and dip them into the syrup for two or three seconds. South African cooks say it is important to dip the *koeksisters* while they're still hot. This will ensure that they absorb the correct amount of syrup.

6. Remove the *koeksisters* from the syrup and serve.

Cape Minstrel Festival Face Paint

South Africa has a large population of mixed-race people who are commonly called coloured. South Africa's coloured population is made up of the descendants of South Africa's original African inhabitants, as well as the slaves and slave owners of the Colonialist period. Coloured South Africans have a distinct culture with many unique traditions.

One such tradition is the Cape Minstrel Festival, a colorful New Year's Day event. During this festival, neighborhood groups join together to form teams. Each team chooses a name and a set of colors. Participants dress up in fancy satin clothing and paint their faces with bold, colorful designs. They perform musical routines in competitions.

You can paint your face with bright colors like the competitors at the Cape Minstrel Festival. When you are finished, you can even perform a song for your friends and family. You probably know some appropriate music already. Cape Minstrel Festival performers sometimes choose traditional South African music, but as often as not, they perform pop songs or old hits by performers such as Michael Jackson or the Beatles.

Face paint
At least one friend

1. Discuss the colors and designs you want painted on your faces.
2. Take turns painting each other's faces.
3. Choose a song to perform in front of an audience.

Chili Bites

At the Cape Minstrel Festival, people sometimes buy food from sidewalk stands and street vendors. One popular snack is chili bites, deep-fried fritters of chickpea flour, potato, onion, and spices.

Ingredients:

2/3 cup chickpea (or garbanzo bean, or gram) flour
1 tablespoon white flour
1 teaspoon baking powder
1 teaspoon salt
1 teaspoon paprika
2 teaspoons ground coriander
1 teaspoon ground cumin
1 tablespoon chopped cilantro
1–3 diced hot chili peppers, to taste
1 medium onion
1 small potato
1/2 cup water
Vegetable oil for deep frying

Instructions:

1. Combine the chickpea flour, white flour, baking powder, salt, and dry spices in a bowl.

2. Add the cilantro and chili peppers to the bowl.
3. Grate the onion and potato and add them to the bowl.
4. Add the water and mix the batter. It should be very thick and very sticky. If it looks dry, add a bit more water. If it looks runny, add a bit more chickpea flour.
5. Pour about 2 inches of oil into a small pan and, with **an adult**'s help, heat it over medium heat.

Prep time: 20 minutes
Cook time: 30 minutes
Serves: 6

6. Your adult helper should drop large spoonfuls of batter into the hot oil and deep fry the balls of batter. When they are golden brown, move them to a paper towel to cool for 5 to 10 minutes.

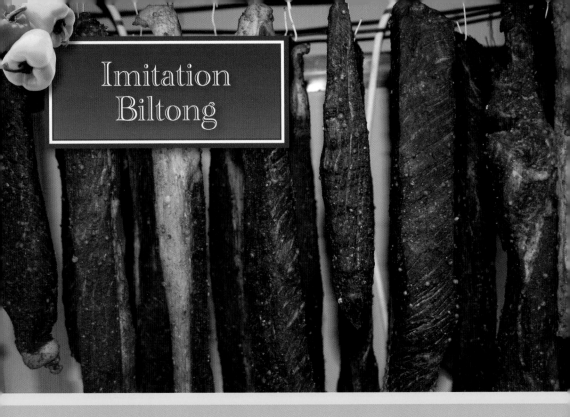

Imitation Biltong

Over time, the white settlers who lived in southern Africa stopped seeing themselves as Europeans. They began calling themselves Afrikaaners, which means "Africans." When the English took control of the Cape Colony from the Dutch in the early 1800s, some Afrikaaners regarded them as foreign invaders. Rather than live under English control, many Afrikaaners moved deeper into the African continent.

Afrikaaners in the African interior faced many challenges. In some ways, their lifestyles were like those of the American pioneers. Their foods were made from simple ingredients that would last a long time. One of these foods was a dried, spiced meat called biltong. Biltong is made from wild game meat or from farmed meat such as beef or ostrich.

Biltong is still very popular in South Africa. People make it by soaking strips of meat in vinegar and spices and hanging them on hooks to dry. It is safe to eat if made properly, but it is possible to make mistakes with the process. Because of this, the traditional recipe for biltong is not included in this book.

Instead, we will start with store-bought beef jerky and spice it with coriander, brown sugar, and black pepper to imitate the flavors of one common biltong recipe. When you buy beef jerky for this recipe, avoid varieties that include strong spices. Instead, choose the most mildly flavored kind you can find. This will allow you to better imitate the flavor of real South African biltong.

Prep time: 10 minutes
Cook time: 30 minutes
Serves: 4

Ingredients:

2 tablespoons whole coriander seeds
1 tablespoon brown sugar
2 teaspoons freshly ground black pepper
½ teaspoon salt
1 tablespoon red wine vinegar
1 package mildly flavored beef jerky

Instructions:

1. Crush the coriander seeds slightly. Use a mortar and pestle if you own one. If not, crush the spices in a bowl using the back of a spoon. You do not need to grind the seeds fine; just break them down so they are no longer whole.
2. Mix the coriander with the sugar, spices, and vinegar.
3. Remove the beef jerky from the package and coat it liberally with your coriander mixture.
4. Lay the jerky on a cookie sheet and, with **an adult**'s help, place it in the oven at 250°F for 30 minutes, or until dry.

Chicken Curry

From the 1800s through the early 1900s, many people immigrated to South Africa from India. Like South Africa's other cultural groups, Indians have made their mark on South African cooking. Indian dishes that made their way into the ordinary South African diet often have a slight twist.

If you have tried chicken curry in the past, you will find this recipe a little different. Like many South African dishes, this one contains a little sugar and cinnamon. This sweet, spicy kick is one of the signatures of South African cooking.

Ingredients:

1 pound boneless chicken breasts
3 tablespoons butter or vegetable oil
1 large onion
1 green bell pepper
1–2 hot chili peppers (optional, to taste)
1 tablespoon curry powder
½ teaspoon turmeric
1 teaspoon ground coriander
½ teaspoon cinnamon
½ teaspoon sugar
½ teaspoon black pepper
1 teaspoon salt
3 cups water
Rice cooked according to package directions

Instructions:

1. Chop the chicken breasts into small pieces and, with **an adult**'s help, brown them in a large pot using half of the butter or oil. When they are well browned, remove them from the pot and set them to one side.

2. Chop the onions and, again with **an adult**'s help, cook them in the rest of the butter for 5 to 8 minutes.

3. While the onions are cooking, chop the bell pepper and the chili peppers, if you are using them.

4. When the onions look clear, return the chicken to the pot. Add the vegetables, spices, and water. Ask **an adult** to bring the pot to a boil.

5. Turn down the heat under the pan and simmer all the ingredients together, covered, for 20 to 30 minutes.

6. Serve over rice.

> **Prep time: 20 minutes**
> **Cook time: 40 minutes**
> **Serves: 4**

Bunny Chow

Today, people of all races have equal rights in South Africa, but that was not always the case. For several centuries, European settlers and their descendants saw themselves as superior to their dark-skinned neighbors. Without allowing black, Indian, or coloured South Africans to take part in the government, white South Africans made laws that gave themselves all the power. In 1948, an all-white government expanded these laws into a system called apartheid. Under apartheid, people of South Africa's many races had to live and work separately. White South Africans were given the best land, the best educational opportunities, and the best jobs.

Under apartheid, black South Africans were allowed to come into white parts of the city only if they worked there. Like anyone, black workers got hungry at lunchtime, but they were not allowed to eat in the restaurants or even to take restaurant dishes outside so that they could eat on the streets. In the 1950s, before the use of plastic takeout containers became common, this caused a problem. How could the black workers eat?

The solution—a unique South African street food called bunny chow—was invented in the city of Durban. Local legend says an Indian shopkeeper, called a *banai,* began hollowing out loaves of bread and filling them with curry. The bread acted as an edible container that was easy to eat on the street. Nobody is quite sure why this food got the strange name bunny chow, but most people think the *bunny* part might be a mispronunciation of *banai.*

Today, South Africans are allowed to eat wherever they want, regardless of their skin color. However, bunny chow—often shortened to just *bunny*—remains popular because it is tasty, inexpensive, and easy to eat on the go.

Prep time: 20 minutes
Cook time: 40 minutes
Serves: 4

Ingredients:

2 large onions
3 tablespoons butter or vegetable oil
1 pound vegetables of your choice, such as
    cauliflower, carrots, squash, peas, or corn
1–2 hot chili peppers (optional, to taste)
3 cups water
1 tablespoon curry powder
½ teaspoon turmeric
1 teaspoon ground coriander
½ teaspoon cinnamon
½ teaspoon sugar
½ teaspoon black pepper
Salt to taste
An unsliced loaf of bread (or deli rolls)

Instructions:

1. Chop the onions and, with **an adult**'s help, cook them in a large
   pot in the butter or oil for 5 to 8 minutes, until they look clear.

South Africa Recipe

2. While the onions are cooking, chop the other vegetables into 1-inch pieces. (If they are already small, like peas, you can skip this step.) Dice the hot chili peppers, if you are using them.

3. Add the vegetables, spices, and other ingredients (except the bread) to the onions, and ask **an adult** to bring the pot to a boil.

4. Turn down the heat under the pan and simmer all the ingredients together, covered, for 20 to 30 minutes.

5. While the curry is cooking, prepare the bread container. Using a sharp knife, cut your loaf of bread into quarters. Carefully cut the soft center out of each piece of bread and set it aside, making lidless containers for food. Leave about half an inch around the edges untouched.

6. Place each bread bowl on a plate, and fill it with hot curry. Spoon the curry onto the hollowed-out piece of bread, and enjoy the tasty chow.

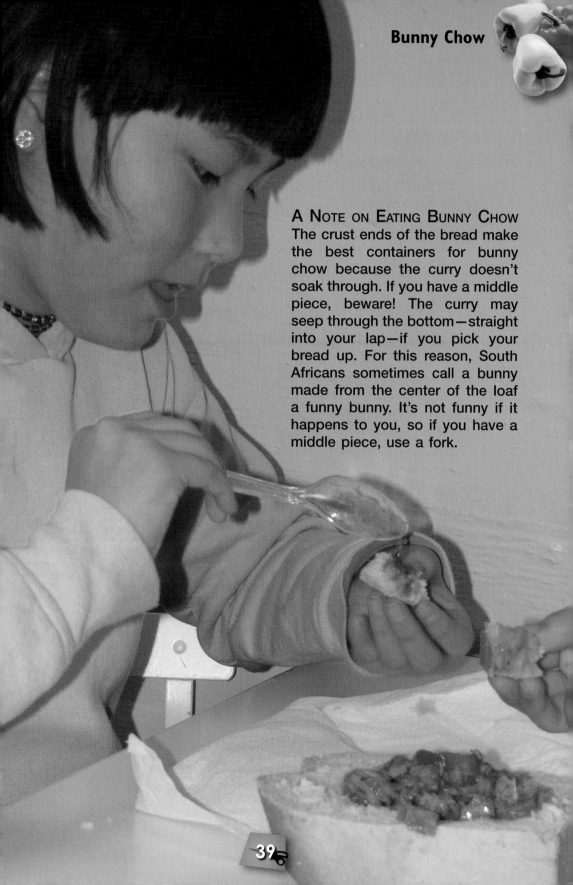

Bunny Chow

A NOTE ON EATING BUNNY CHOW
The crust ends of the bread make the best containers for bunny chow because the curry doesn't soak through. If you have a middle piece, beware! The curry may seep through the bottom—straight into your lap—if you pick your bread up. For this reason, South Africans sometimes call a bunny made from the center of the loaf a funny bunny. It's not funny if it happens to you, so if you have a middle piece, use a fork.

Bead Flower

Although apartheid is no longer in place, non-white South Africans remain poorer on average than white South Africans. Many were poorly educated during apartheid and have few job skills that can gain them steady work. Some people in this situation become artists, making crafts to sell to the many tourists who pass through South Africa every year. Bead sculpture is one of the most popular art forms.

Materials:

Memory wire or solid-core electrical wire, about 3 feet long
100 beads, any color
Green electrical tape

Instructions:

1. About 6 to 8 inches from one end of your wire, make a ½-inch loop. This will form the center of your flower.
2. To strengthen the center of your flower, thread the long end of your wire through the loop and pull it tight. Repeat this process five or six times, twisting the wire around the loop (see photo).
3. To make the first petal, thread about twenty small beads onto the wire in any color pattern of your choice. Then make a loop of the beaded section and twist the end around the center of the flower to secure it.
4. Follow step 3 four more times to make the rest of the petals.
5. When you are finished with your petals, wind the excess wire around the stem to strengthen it.
6. Wrap the stem with green tape.

Recycled Paper Baskets

Like beading, weaving is a common craft in South Africa. People who make baskets and bags to sell to tourists often use materials they can find for free. They use grass and sticks they cut themselves, or they use materials other people throw away.

You can make a woven basket out of recycled paper. Consider using an outdated map, old newspapers, used wrapping paper, or leftover paper from some other project. Almost anything will do, as long as it is large and colorful. When you have chosen your paper, follow the instructions below to make a simple four-sided basket.

Materials:

1 or 2 large sheets of used paper
Scissors
A pencil
A ruler or yardstick
White glue

Instructions:

1. Cut sixteen strips of paper. Make each strip about 15 inches long and 3 to 4 inches wide.
2. Fold the strips lengthwise to make 1-inch strips. Folded strips are stronger, which makes them easier to weave and harder to tear.

3. On a table, lay five strips of paper side by side in the color pattern of your choice.

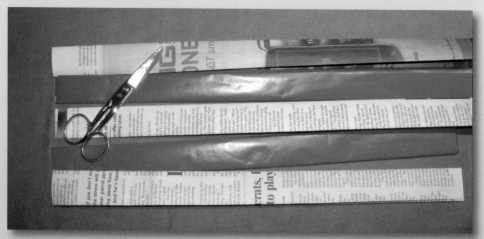

4. Interweave these strips with five more strips, going in the opposite direction. You should end up with a pile of interlocked paper that looks like a plus sign. The center of the plus will be the bottom of your basket. Each arm of the plus will become a side.

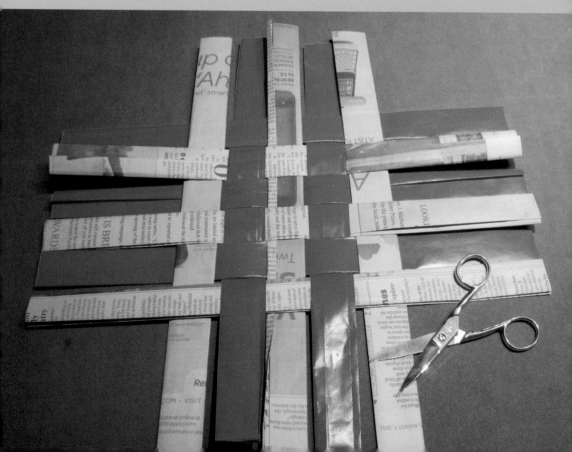

5. If your strips slip around, glue them in place with a small dot of glue in each overlapped corner of your plus sign. This will hold the pieces in place as you work on the sides.

6. Cut the six remaining strips in half. Take three of the short strips and interweave them with the loose ends on one side of your plus. Trim two of these strips so that they fit the length of the basket's side. Leave the final strip a little long.

7. Repeat step 6 with the other three sides of the plus sign.

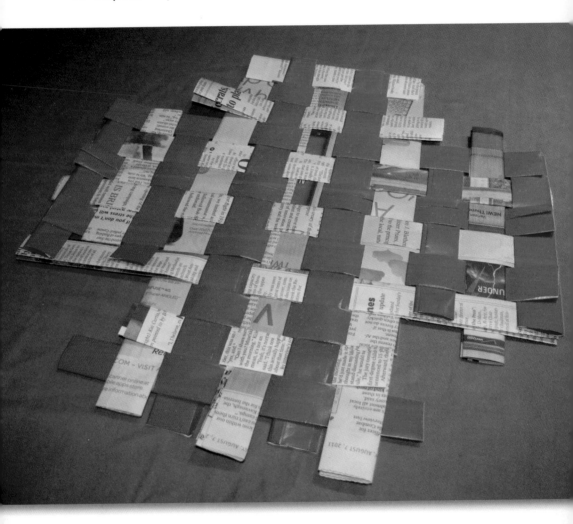

8. Fold up the sides. On the end of each long side piece, place a dot of glue. Glue it to the inside of the side next to it. This will hold up the sides of your basket.

9. At this point you should have a four-sided basket, with the ends of your original ten strips poking up. Trim these to make them even, and cover them with excess paper to give the finished basket a neater appearance.

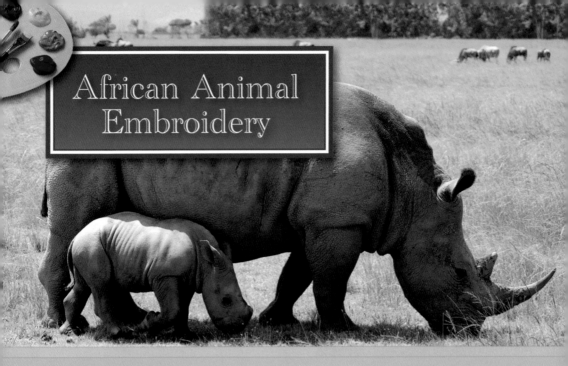

African Animal Embroidery

Large African animals once roamed free throughout South Africa. Today they remain only in the largest national parks. Under apartheid, black South Africans were not allowed to visit the parks and see these beautiful animals. Since the transition to democracy, South Africa's national parks have been open to everyone. They are an important part of South Africa's economy because they provide jobs for tour guides, restaurant workers, hotel workers, and craftspeople. You can embroider the outline of an African animal onto a unique greeting card to give to a friend or family member.

Materials:

Plain paper
Pen or pencil
1 piece of colorful card stock
   (8½ inches by 5½ inches)
1 piece of thick cardboard
4–5 paper clips
1 pushpin
Heavy colored thread
Scissors
Sewing needle
Colored markers
White glue

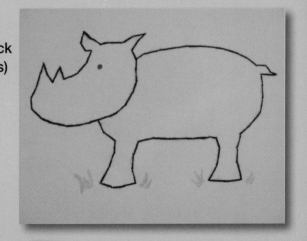

Thumbtacks

1. On a sheet of white paper, draw or trace the outline of the
   African animal you want to embroider on the front of your card.
   You will be stitching this picture onto the card, so don't add
   fancy shading, faces, or body patterns. You can draw these
   parts later.
2. Fold your thick card stock paper down the middle to make it
   into the shape of a card.
3. Place your card facedown on the cardboard. Paper clip it in
   place so that it will not move.

4. Lay your African animal picture on the card. If you're making a card that folds at the left, place the picture to the right of the fold. If you're making a card that folds at the top, place the picture below the fold. Secure it with the paper clips.

5. Using the pushpin, poke holes through your picture and the card, into the cardboard underneath. Make the holes about ¼ inch apart. When you are finished, remove the card and pattern from the cardboard backing. Discard the pattern and put the paper clips away.

6. Now it's time to stitch the picture onto the front of the card. Cut a piece of thread about 4 feet long and thread your needle. Pull the thread through so that its two ends meet. Make a knot at the end of the thread.

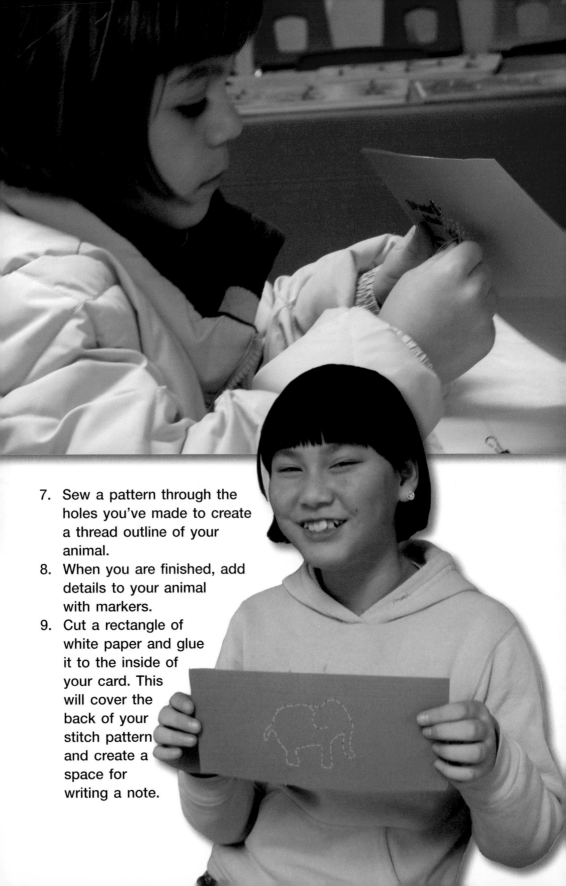

7. Sew a pattern through the holes you've made to create a thread outline of your animal.

8. When you are finished, add details to your animal with markers.

9. Cut a rectangle of white paper and glue it to the inside of your card. This will cover the back of your stitch pattern and create a space for writing a note.

Lamb Braai

In the early 1990s, apartheid laws were abolished, and South Africa held its first democratic elections. The first black president, Nelson Mandela (who spent 27 years in prison for his role as a freedom fighter during apartheid), could have taken revenge on the white Afrikaaners who had oppressed him and his people for so many years. Instead, Mandela encouraged all South Africans to learn to live together in peace.

Mandela wanted South Africans of every race to adopt some traditions from each other. One of the outcomes of this effort was National Braai Day, held on September 24 every year. The braai, or barbecue, is an Afrikaaner food tradition that other South Africans have picked up—partly at Mandela's urging, and partly because it is fun.

South Africans braai all kinds of meat and sausages as well as vegetables. One common dish to braai is lamb chops. For this recipe, you will need to plan ahead. The lamb chops should marinate in spices for one day before you braai them.

Prep time: 15 minutes
the day before,
about 60 minutes
on braai day
Cook time: 10 minutes
Serves: 4

½ orange
½ onion
½ tablespoon brown sugar
1 tablespoon oil
1 teaspoon salt
½ teaspoon pepper
4 lamb chops

Instructions:

1. The day before your braai, place the lamb chops in a baking dish. Grate the peel off half an orange and squeeze out the juice as well. Put the peel and juice into the baking dish with the lamb, oil, and spices.
2. Cover the lamb chops and place them in a refrigerator overnight.
3. About an hour before you want to eat, ask **an adult** to help you light some charcoal in a barbecue. Wait until the coals are ready for cooking.
4. With the help of **an adult**, place the lamb chops on the barbecue.
5. Depending on the thickness of the lamb chops and the heat of the coals, the meat will need to cook for about 2 to 5 minutes on each side.
6. When the chops are done, ask the **adult** to remove them from the grill. Let them rest for 5 to 10 minutes before eating.

Homemade Soccer Ball

In 2010, South Africa hosted the FIFA World Cup soccer tournament. In the process, South Africa became the first African country to host a major international sporting event. The country was swept with soccer fever. People didn't just watch soccer; they also played soccer. If they didn't have the money to afford a store-bought soccer ball, they just made their own!

Many African kids are experts at making balls. Their methods vary widely, depending on their desires and the available materials, but the balls are usually made of some wadded-up discarded material wrapped tightly with nylon, twine, or rubber bands. Homemade soccer balls tend to be small, about half the size of a regular soccer ball.

Materials:

A wad of plastic grocery bags
    or cloth rags
Strong twine or rubber bands

Instructions:

1. Ball up your bags or cloth as tightly as you can. To do this, start with a small amount of material and squish it down. Add more material and squish that, too. Continue this process until you have a small, dense ball.
2. Tie your ball together with twine or rubber bands. Make them as tight as you can without breaking them. If you are using twine, weave it around the ball to make an interlocking pattern. If you are using rubber bands, tie them around from several angles so that the ball is held securely.

Fish and Chips

All Foods Strictly Halaal   drink   Coca-Cola

Prep time: 30 minutes
Cook time: 45 minutes
Serves: 4

Naturally, fans at the World Cup got hungry. Many visited small shops that sell fish and chips, a popular dish that English settlers contributed to South African cuisine. In South Africa, this dish is traditionally made with locally harvested fish such as hake or snoek. These fish varieties are generally unavailable in the United States, so you will need to choose a variety of white fish such as halibut, cod, or haddock.

Ingredients:

Chips
4 potatoes
Vegetable oil for frying
Salt
White vinegar (optional)

Fish

1 cup flour + a few teaspoons
   additional flour
½ teaspoon baking powder
½ teaspoon salt
½ teaspoon black pepper
½ cup water
½ cup milk
4 white fish fillets
Oil for frying
White vinegar (optional)

Instructions:

1. Preheat the oven to 400°F.
2. Peel the potatoes (or leave the skins on if you want) and slice them into ½-inch-wide strips.

South Africa Recipe

3. Spread the potatoes out in a single layer on a cookie sheet and coat them liberally with vegetable oil, using about ½ to ¾ cup for the pan.

4. Ask **an adult** to help you place the cookie sheet in the oven.

5. Bake the potato strips for about 15 to 20 minutes, until they are golden brown on one side. With **an adult**'s help, carefully remove the cookie sheet from the oven and turn the strips over. Have the **adult** return them to the oven to bake for an additional 15 minutes, or until the other side is golden brown.

6. After you turn the potatoes over, begin mixing the batter for the fish. Combine 1 cup flour, baking powder, salt, pepper, water, and milk.

7. Pat the fish fillets dry with a paper towel and sprinkle them on both sides with flour. This will help the batter to stick to the fish.

8. Dredge the fish in the batter until it is well coated. While you do this, ask **an adult** to put about 2 inches of oil into a medium-sized frying pan and heat it over medium heat.

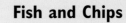

9. When the oil is hot, ask your adult helper to drop the battered fish fillets into the pan. Fry the fish for 5 to 8 minutes. Turn it over halfway through the cooking process if necessary.

10. Drain the fish on a paper towel. If you wish, sprinkle both the fish and the chips with salt and vinegar before serving.

Vuvuzela

No sporting event in South Africa is complete without vuvuzelas—long plastic horns that fans blow constantly before, during, and after their favorite sporting events. Ever since the 2010 World Cup made vuvuzelas popular in other countries, it has been possible to buy them over the Internet and at some toy stores. But why buy a horn when you can make your own?

Materials:

2 cardboard paper towel tubes
Heavy duty scissors
Clear tape
1 disposable drinking cup
Colored electrical tape in the colors of your favorite sports team

Instructions:

1. Join the paper towel tubes to make one long tube. To do this, make a small slit at the end of one tube, fold the end to taper it slightly, and insert it into the next tube. Use clear tape to hold the tubes together.
2. To make the bell end of the horn, cut about 5 to 6 slits at one end of your long tube. Each slit should be about 2 inches long.
3. Cut the bottom out of the disposable drinking cup.
4. Insert the small end of the cup into the slit ends of the tube, and fasten the cup into place with clear tape.
5. Use colored electrical tape to decorate your horn in the colors of your favorite sports team.

Further Reading

Books

Blauer, Ettagale, and Jason Lauré. *South Africa.* New York: Children's Press, 2006.

Cornell, Kari. *Cooking the Southern African Way.* Minneapolis: Lerner Publications Company, 2005.

Koosmann, Melissa. *Meet Our New Student from South Africa.* Hockessin, DE: Mitchell Lane Publishers, 2009.

———. *The Fall of Apartheid in South Africa.* Hockessin, DE: Mitchell Lane Publishers, 2009.

Wagner, Lisa. *Cool African Cooking: Fun and Tasty Recipes for Kids.* Edina, MN: ABDO Publishing, 2011.

Stories

Naidoo, Beverly. *Journey to Jo'burg: A South African Story.* New York: HarperTrophy, 1998.

———. *No Turning Back: A Novel of South Africa.* New York: HarperCollins Publishers, 1997.

Paton, Alan. *Cry, the Beloved Country.* New York: Scribner, 2003.

Works Consulted

Byrnes, Rita M., ed. *South Africa: A Country Study.* Washington: GPO for the Library of Congress, 1996.

CIA World Factbook. "South Africa." https://www.cia.gov/library/publications/the-world-factbook/geos/sf.html

Fitzgerald, Diane. *Zulu-Inspired Beadwork: Weaving Techniques and Projects.* Foreword by Richard Green. Loveland, CO: Interweave Books, 2007.

Morris, Jean, and Eleanor Preston-Whyte. *Speaking With Beads: Zulu Arts from Southern Africa.* New York: Thames and Hudson, 1994.

Skotnes, Pippa. *Claim to the Country: The Archive of Wilhelm Bleek and Lucy Lloyd.* Johannesburg, South Africa: Jacana, 2007.

Van Wyk, Magdalene. *The Complete South African Cookbook.* Johannesburg: Central News Agency, Ltd., 2001.

On the Internet

2010 FIFA World Cup South Africa
   http://www.fifa.com/worldcup/archive/southafrica2010/index.html

Ancient San Rock Art
   http://www.historyforkids.org/learn/africa/art/san.htm

Find North by Finding the North Star
   http://www.wilderness-survival-skills.com/finding-the-north-star.html

The History of the Sextant
   http://pwifland.tripod.com/historysextant/

National Geographic Kids: South Africa
   http://kids.nationalgeographic.com/kids/places/find/south-africa/

Photo Gallery: Cape Town Carnival
   http://johnedwinmason.typepad.com/photos/cape_town_new_years_carni/index.html

South African History Online
   http://www.sahistory.org.za/

Time for Kids Around the World: South Africa
   http://www.timeforkids.com/TFK/teachers/aw/wr/main/0,28132,590829,00.html

Glossary

banai (bah-NAHY)—An Indian shopkeeper in the South African city of Durban.

Bantu (BAN-too)-**speaking people**—Several related groups of Africans who speak similar languages. Some Bantu-speaking people moved into southern Africa around 500 CE.

biltong (BIL-tahng)—Dried, spiced meat.

braai (BRY)—Barbecue (noun and verb).

bunny chow—Curry served in a hollowed-out piece of bread.

chickpea flour—Flour made from dried chickpeas; sometimes called garbanzo bean flour.

chili bites—A snack made from chickpea flour, onions, potatoes, and spices.

coloured people—South Africans of mixed racial descent. This term is common in South African English, but it is not used in American English.

coriander (KOR-ee-an-der)—Dried seeds of the coriander plant, used as a spice.

corrugated (KOR-uh-gay-tid)—Shaped from parallel folds and ridges.

corrugation (kor-uh-GAY-shun)—A fold or ridge on a corrugated surface.

cumin (KYOO-min)—Seeds of the cumin herb, used as a spice.

equator (ee-KWAY-ter)—An imaginary line around the center of the earth, equally distant from the north and south poles.

koeksister (KOOK-sis-ter)—Deep-fried Cape Malay doughnuts.

mielie pap (MEE-lee POP)—A thick porridge made from cornmeal flour, a common side dish in South African cuisine; it is also called pap.

millet (MIL-it)—Any of several small-grained crops that people grow as food or animal feed.

North Star—The bright star Polaris (poh-LAYR-iss) that is visible from northern skies. It is lined up with the axis of Earth, so hikers and sailors use it to find north.

San (SAHN)—The earliest known group of people to inhabit southern Africa.

sextant (SEK-stent)—An instrument used for measuring angles with the horizon.

staple (STAY-pul)—One of the main foods in a given diet.

thatch—A roofing material made of dry grass or reeds.

turmeric (TER-mer-ik)—A tropical plant used for seasoning and for making yellow dye.

vuvuzela (voo-voo-ZAY-luh)—A long plastic horn South African sports fans often blow at sporting events.

Zulu (ZOO-loo)—A member of a Bantu-speaking South African group.

Index

ABOUT THE
AUTHOR

Melissa Koosmann (back, center) studied creative writing at Linfield College in Oregon and at the University of Arizona. She spent several years teaching community college English classes and working with university students with learning disabilities.

Melissa and her husband lived in Cape Town, South Africa, from 2008 to 2010. She traveled extensively through the country, learning everything she could about the land and people, and sampling every new kind of food she could find. She took a cooking class at a local Indian restaurant, bought handmade crafts from street hawkers, and—best of all—tutored kids at a local elementary school. She and her husband now reside in Seattle, Washington.